AF375423

My Satori

Karen Hanson

Copyright © 2023 by Karen Hanson

All rights reserved. This book or any portion thereof may not be reproduced or used in any manner whatsoever without the express written permission of the publisher except for the use of brief quotations in a book review.

Welcome!
Satori means
seeing into one's
true nature.
I humbly share
My Satori
with you.

I am a global citizen, inviting all people to unite in love for each other and the planet.

I wish I was an angel. I would sit with you and listen to your heart's stories. Then I would show you Heaven.

Kneel and you

will be closer to

Mother Earth

who is chanting

to the drumbeat

of Justice.

Life comes to me
in fragments.
I weave a
tapestry from the
particles of rich
and colorful
moments. This
is what I choose.

I looked for a
palace and then I
came across a
shieling. I found
my people there.
The palace
no longer calls
my name.

I am blinded by
the light of glory
that shines into
my window early
mornings,
reminding me of
new beginnings.

Come and sit
beside me. We
will break bread
and breathe in
the gentle breath
of life until we
fly again.

Love is
extraordinary. It
lives in each one of
us to be
resurrected with
abundant certainty
at just the right
moments.

Truth has a life
of its own. If we
watch closely,
listen carefully,
and speak clearly,
then truth makes
itself known.

I am a simple
being moving
through life
looking for my
shadow that
reminds there
will be light
along the way.

Season after
season, the
majestic pine
bears the weight
of the snow
blanket who is
her teacher.

I am a
tumbleweed.
Wind-catching
branches and
samples of
earth's treasures
become a part of
me. I am with
Mother Earth.

The children
warriors are
gathering and
their voices
are united.
They will
succeed where
we have failed.

When I reach
for God I feel
connected. I am
grounded in
faith while
catching a ride
on a skyhook to
Heaven.

When no one is
watching, think
of life as
watching you.
Soar and seek to
be a free and
fierce warrior.

Mother Ocean

and Father Sky,

I say your name.

Watch over me as

I pass through

these endless

waters and open

fields of grass.

Harsh

sensibilities

shatter dreams.

Join me as we

embrace

possibilities.

We can do this!

Standing

on

the

edge

of

the

moon

The White
Hawk flew just
close enough so
I could catch
a ride and travel
to places I
have never
been before.

While canoeing down a river, I invited a stranger to join me. I offered up, "Get ready for the ride of your life!"

I journeyed
through the
hinterland and
discovered who I
am. As I
return to the
heartland, I am
at peace.

Come and walk through the weeds with me. We will experience imperfections, raw reflections, and deep rooted feelings that make us who we are.

If you keep

dodging justice,

she will find you

with her relentless

spirit. At the

end of the day,

she will rise.

Today I do not

speak. I bow my

head while

lifting my palms

toward the

heavens, and

I simply

pray for peace.

If your heart is
hurting, I wish
to offer mine. It
is not much better,
but it is
mine to offer.

Lone Traveler,
Gather your belongings
and haversack. Cross
the plains and
go where the
bedded forester
feathergrass
leads you.

Take the halyard

firmly in your

hands and hoist

the sail at life's

end. The breeze

will take you

home, my friend.

If we search hard
enough, we will
discover the likes
of the beauty
of the lavender
blush wood from
the Bubinga tree
in Africa.

Try stepping
into the lane
of passion and
purpose and
see where it
takes you. What
are you
waiting for?

What we do
matters the
degree, but
with no mend
to offer, our
silence is
our speak.

Gather planks
of wood from
the fields; some
that are flawless
and some that
are not. We
will build this
house together.

I saw a
Keel-billed
Toucan. I
would have
missed her
magnificence if
I had not
looked up.

Whatever lies

ahead, you will

be stronger,

wiser, and better

for stepping

into it as opposed

to stepping

away from it.

Integrity is the
most precious
gift that guides
us through our
journey and
becomes the
protagonist in
our story.

I walked on the
surface of the
moon today.
They said it was
impossible for
me. How do they
explain the
moondust in
my hair?

I set a place at
my table for
newborns to come
and for those who
have moved on. I
will set these
places at my table
from now on.

Music for the
dance inspires
me to move,
but my feet
have a mind of
their own. I
dance anyway.

Healing waters

flow while

sending forth

God-speak

blessings that

dance above

our heads.

I am a single
blip in the
universe
claiming my
space.

Each of us
has our own
story to tell,
burden to carry,
or a hurt to
reveal.
Together
we heal.

For the angler

who casts from

mid-stream is

it for the quest

or the catch?

Perhaps the aim

lies somewhere

in-between.

We are no
longer strangers
when we dance
on the street to
the sounds of
brotherhood,
justice, and joy.

On the stage or
in the street
Spoken Word
and people meet.
Langston Hughes
draws a crowd.
Word play to be
read aloud.

Step off the path
and explore
tributaries. They
will lead you to
confluences in
your life. You will
be better for it.

The spirit calls
out my name,
and this is what
I do when
broken and
confused.
I fly.
I still fly.

*Wishing comes
to life in a place
where dreams
are realized.*

Pay attention
and lend a hand.
Offer time
because we can.
Time is
free to spend.

On the 18th hole,

we reflect on our

passion for the

try and putt for

the last time.

Tomorrow comes,

and we tee off again.

Balance and
bend. Overcome
and do not
give in.
You will survive.

The crossroad

is behind

me now. What

lies ahead is a

single path

to Nirvana.

Energy is molded by the love in our hearts that goes beyond the boundaries of common thoughts and conversations.

I looked

into the rearview

mirror and I

am at peace

moving forward

knowing where

I have been.

Introduce me
to your most
intimate friends
so I can see
you through
their eyes.

I sat on the

stoop and waited

for you. How

was I supposed

to know that

you were

already here?

Give wings to the
right side of
justice and she
will soar like the
Phoenix rising.

As they raised the barn, the townsfolk understood their devotion to each other and the land.

The Peregrine flew
high above
the Great Plains
today. As
she soared,
she called out
my name.

Today I walk
with my sisters
and brothers on
the path of social
justice. We
shall not pause.

Tonight the

moon is red and

the planet is on

fire. Mother

Earth cries out

to us wishing

to be heard.

Who owns the
air I ride? Who
makes the rules as
I glide? Dust to
dust is what
they'd have
me be, but
fly I must.

In the dust bowl,
I came across a
seedling and knew
that tomorrow
would bring a new
crop of hope and
promise to
my people.

I can barely
see the flickering
of light from
the house down
the road. It
reminds me
that I am
not alone.

I have been
beating this
drum forever.
The day I stop
will be the day
my heart stops.

You cradled
me when
I was young,
and now I
cradle you. Let
us embrace the
roundabout of life.

Haven't we
been down this
road before?
Until we are
free, we will walk
down this road
once more.

What is life
without passion?
It is not
standing still
while contemplating
the next move.

Catch the train
if you can. It
may not come by
here again.

Love more
powerful than
anger, compassion
more compelling
than indifference,
and acceptance
more worthy
than resistance.

I am whole with
my particle family
and all that is
good with life. I
am complete and
a welcomed
passenger on the
wings of the wind.

There are many avenues to get to where you are headed. Take the road less traveled and keep your headlights on.

Youngins,
Embrace this
moment in
history and carry
the banner
of hope, faith,
and freedom.
You are strong
and we are weak.

When you think
no one is watching,
life is watching
you. Dance like you
have never danced
before, and show
them who you are.

A heavy
heart and a
hopeful spirit
line the fabric
of my soul. I
shall survive
and thrive
once again.

As a young
girl, I watched
the train-
travelers and
I wished I was
one of them.
Catch a
ride and fly.

In this room,
immigrants,
preachers,
scientists, and
non-believers
come together.

www.ingramcontent.com/pod-product-compliance
Lightning Source LLC
Chambersburg PA
CBHW040731120726
48010CB00002B/83